THE ROYAL NAVY IN FOCUS 1970 - 1979

Compiled by Lt Cdr Ben Warlow Royal Navy

£14.95

EDITOR'S NOTES

The 1970s saw a major transition in the ships of the Royal Navy. The last of the wartime vessels, often modernised and adapted beyond recognition in order to carry the latest weapons and sensors, or used for training or trials, were still in service, whilst newer ships were in full production. The most significant step forward was in the change of propulsion systems. The first gas turbine experiments at sea had been in coastal forces vessels, and then, in tandem with steam plants in most instances, in frigates and destroyers. With technical problems ironed out, the fleet was fast becoming totally reliant on this mode of propulsion, with steam plants disappearing rapidly. Similarly, the last few ships with direct current electrical systems were already earmarked for disposal.

The major emphasis on ship construction had been on frigates, with the evolution of the Whitby class through to the Leanders. At the end of the period covered the first Type 22, the BROADSWORD, had just been completed. The construction of major war vessels had been almost minimal during the previous few years, but the Invincible Class Through Deck Cruisers/aircraft carriers were on the stocks - and the first would be completed only just in time to take part in the Falklands War. Minecountermeasures vessels had been built in bulk in the 50s, and it would be a while before the Hunts and Rivers appeared at sea as long awaited replacements for the ageing Ton class vessels. Submarine development and construction had been progressed, with a steady stream of both nuclear and conventional vessels joining the Fleet. The Navy had taken on the deterrent role, and were to maintain it in its traditionally silent manner throughout the 70s. The conventional submarine design had reached a peak with the Porpoises, which had been repeated with the O Class, whilst nuclear "killer" submarines were improving in ability and performance by leaps and bounds. With the withdrawal from bases abroad, more emphasis was being placed on the self sufficiency of warships backed by the Royal Fleet Auxiliaries.

The photographs here are mostly those taken by Official RN photographers, supplemented with some private shots (credits on page 160). Although every endeavour has been made to weed out photographs taken outside this period, occasionally it has been necessary to include the odd photograph taken earlier or later in order to keep the balance between types of ships, and to ensure that certain ships which served during the period covered are not omitted.

A colour section has been included, though most warships in their grey paint against a grey sea and sky still show up better in black and white; and colour photography at sea in the 1970s was limited.

What is not visible from the photographs here is the remarkable change in living conditions onboard the ships that was taking place at this time. Dining Halls had become standard, as had bunks, air conditioning and plenty of fresh water. The rum issue had come to an end at the start of this period (1970). Perhaps the Old Salts will consider that "It did not blow as it used to", and that sailors had gone soft (a cry of most generations) - but the Navy had become more technical and warfare had come to depend far more on electrical sensors than human eyesight etc. Nevertheless, those who were to serve in the older vessels during this period and who did not benefit from the habitability improvements often look back at the time with fond memories, and were proud of their rather old fashioned ships, which often had a more dashing, punchy appearance than the more modern vessels.

It is hoped that this snapshot of the Royal Navy in transition will appeal to the many who have enjoyed the previous books in this series, and also to new readers, all of whom I hope will find many hours of interesting browsing

Ben Warlow
Burnham On Crouch 1998

HMS ACHILLES

The Leander Class frigate ACHILLES was completed by Yarrow 9/6/70. One of the last of her class, she was never modernised and retained her 4.5 inch turret to the end of her career. In 1975 she evacuated refugees from Vietnam. Later that year her bows were damaged in a collision with a supertanker in the Dover Straits. She undertook Cod War patrols in 1976 and in 1977 supported the Belize garrison. She was in the Orient Express deployment during 1983, and became part of the Dartmouth Training Squadron in 1989. Paid off 1/90 and sold to Chile, renamed MINISTRO ZENTENO and carried to Chile on a heavy lift ship.

HMS ACTIVE

The ACTIVE was a Type 21 frigate built by Vosper Thornycroft. She commissioned 17/6/77 after a delay awaiting components for her Exocet missile system. The next year she assisted with oil pollution operations in the North Sea when the Greek tanker ELENE V was cut in half by another vessel. In 1979 she helped evacuate refugees from Gulf ports after disturbances ashore. She took part in the Falklands War, carrying out gunfire support for the final assault on Port Stanley. In 1988 she provided hurricane relief in Jamaica. Sold to the Pakistan Navy 23/9/94 and renamed SHAH JAHAN.

HMS AJAX

One of the first Leander Class frigates, she was laid down as the Rothesay class FOWEY, and completed by Cammell Laird 10/12/63. She was originally fitted with 40 mm guns aft as the Seacat missile systems were not then available. Her first few years were spent in the Far East. In 1970-73 she underwent a long refit at Devonport, having her 4.5 inch turret replaced by an Ikara anti-submarine missile system. Seacat missiles were fitted aft, but 40mm guns were also mounted amidships. She paid off 30/5/85, became a harbour training ship at Devonport prior to being towed to Millom for breaking up 2/88.

HMS ALACRITY

The ALACRITY was a Type 21 frigate built by Yarrow and completed 2/4/77. During the Falklands War she sank the Argentine auxiliary ISLA DE LOS ESTADOS during a night action, and carried out a first transit of Falkland Sound to determine whether it was mined. Later she was slightly damaged whilst trying to rescue the crew of the ATLANTIC CONVEYOR. In 1989 she assisted islanders in the West Indies in the wake of hurricane HUGO. She paid off 1/3/94 and was sold to Pakistan, being renamed BADR.

HMS ALBION

The ALBION was built as a Centaur Class aircraft carrier and was completed (after ten years under construction) by Swan Hunter in 05/54. She took part in the Suez campaign and was converted to a Commando Carrier at Portsmouth 1961/62. The lessons from the conversion of her sister ship (BULWARK) had been incorporated, and she could be distinguished by her type 965 radar on the island. She served in the Far East, being involved in the confrontation with Indonesia and the withdrawal from Aden, before being laid up in 1972. She was sold in 10/73 to Wilson Walton Engineering for use as an off-shore crane ship. This never happened and she was resold in 11/73 and broken up at Faslane.

HMS ALFRISTON

The ALFRISTON was one of the first Ton Class minesweepers built and launched by Thornycroft 29/4/53. She was used by the RNR under the names WARSASH (1954-60) and KILMOREY (1960-76). She then joined the Fishery Protection Squadron for 2 years before rejoining the RNR in the 10th MCMS (Solent Division). She paid off in 1986 and was towed to Bruges 12/88 for breaking up.

HMS AMAZON

The Type 21 frigate AMAZON was the first of her class, being completed by Vosper Thornycroft 2/5/74. Shortly after completion 350 tons of ballast had to be installed to counter topweight. She suffered an engine room fire in the Far East in 1977. She had underwater damage when she struck an uncharted pinnacle in the Far East in 1980. In 1983 her hull was externally strengthened as a result of cracking in severe weather. She paid off 31/7/93 and was sold to Pakistan and renamed BABUR.

HMS ANDREW

The ANDREW was completed 16/03/48 by Vickers-Armstrong at Barrow. The A class had been designed for Pacific operations and were of all welded construction. In 1953 she became the first submarine to cross the Atlantic, both ways, submerged. She was modernised with a streamlined hull, but still retained a gun, the last RN submarine to do so. The gun was landed to HMS DOLPHIN before she was broken up at Plymouth in 05/77.

HMS ANTELOPE

The ANTELOPE was a Type 21 frigate, built by Vosper Thornycroft and completed 30/6/75. In 1981 in the West Indies she seized £30 million of marijuana from a cargo vessel. She took part in the Falklands War, being hit by two bombs off San Carlos, one of which blew up during efforts to defuse it. One man was lost in the attack, and another in the explosion, which sank the ship 24/05/82.

HMS ANTRIM

The ANTRIM was the last of the County Class guided missile destroyers built when completed by Fairfields 14/7/70. She was later fitted with Exocet in place of her second 4.5 inch turret. She led the force that recaptured South Georgia in April 1982, and was hit by a bomb (which did not explode) during the action to recapture the Falklands, but continued to operate. In 1983 she stood by off Grenada during a crisis on the island. She was sold to Chile, renamed ALMIRANTE COCHRANE and sailed from Portsmouth on 29/6/84.

HMS APOLLO

The APOLLO was the penultimate Leander Class frigate, built by Yarrow and completed 28/1/72. She underwent none of the major modifications carried out on her sisters during her lifetime. She undertook Cod War patrols in 1973, being in collision with the Icelandic gunboat AEGIR 29/8/73. In 1982 she was damaged in severe weather in the South Atlantic. She was sold to Pakistan 13/7/88 and renamed ZULFIQUAR.

F70

HMS ARDENT

The ARDENT was built by Yarrow, completing on 10/9/77. These frigates used gas turbines for both cruising and main propulsion, and could accelerate rapidly to 34 knots. She was damaged in a collision with a merchant ship off Portsmouth 11/77. She was part of the Task Force which recaptured the Falklands when she came under air attack on 22/5/82 while bombarding Goose Green. She was set on fire aft and finally abandoned. 22 of her crew died in the incident.

HMS ARETHUSA

The ARETHUSA was in the first group (narrow beam) of Leander class frigates, completed 29/9/65 by White at Cowes, being one of the first of the class completed with Seacat missiles. She took part in the Cod War in 1973, colliding with the Icelandic gunboat ODINN 10/8/73. She was refitted with Ikara anti-submarine missiles 1974-77 and then with a towed array sonar in 1985. Finally paid off at Portsmouth 4/4/89. She left there 1/6/91 for use as a target after being gutted internally.

HMS ARGONAUT

The ARGONAUT was completed 17/8/67 by Hawthorn Leslie, and was a Y136-boiler fitted Leander with a narrow beam. She escorted the RMS QUEEN MARY on the liner's final voyage to the USA, and then went on to circumnavigate the World. She carried out Beira Patrols in 1971, and Cod War patrols 1973. In 1974 she assisted in the evacuation from Cyprus of British citizens. She was refitted 76-80 with Exocet and Seacat missiles at Devonport. During the Falklands War she was hit by 2 1000 lb bombs which did not explode, but was badly damaged. Towed array sonar was fitted during repairs in 1983. In 7/87 she helped rescue Richard Branson and the crew of the balloon VIRGIN ATLANTIC FLYER off Northern Ireland. Paid off 31.3.93, she was towed from Portsmouth 25/1/95 for breaking up in Spain.

HMS ARIADNE

The ARIADNE was the last of the Leander class frigates to be completed (by Yarrow 28/6/72). She never underwent major modifications and retained her gun turret throughout her service career. She carried out Cod War patrols in 1973. In 1986 she assisted with flood relief in Jamaica. She served in the Dartmouth Training Squadron in 1991 and paid off 4/92, having carried out the last firing from an RN twin gun turret off the Isle of Wight. She was also the last RN ship to fire the Limbo anti-submarine weapon. She was sold to Chile and sailed under the name GENERAL BAQUEDANO 15/6/92.

HMS ARK ROYAL

Laid down during World War II, the ARK ROYAL was not completed until 02/55. Although updated during her construction, she had several major refits during her career to allow her to keep up with advancing technology, a large one being from 03/67 to 02/70 which enabled her to operate Phantom and Buccaneer aircraft. This cost over £32 million and included a new waist catapult, a full 8.5 degree angled deck and new radar. As can be seen in this photograph, her guns had been removed, but she still retained an air of power, being the Royal Navy's largest warship. She paid off in 02/79, and was sold for breaking up in 07/80 at Cairnryan.

HMS ASHANTI

The Tribal class frigate ASHANTI was completed by Yarrow 23/11/61. The class were armed with single 4.5 inch guns retained in store from old destroyers and powered by a combined steam and gas turbine propulsion system driving a single propeller. ASHANTI was fitted with variable depth sonar in 1969. In 1971 she was part of the force covering the evacuation of British Forces from Malta. In 2/74 she lost two men when hit by a freak wave off Bermuda and in 3/77 suffered a boiler room fire in which 3 men died. She paid off for refit, and from 1981-1986 was a harbour training ship at Portsmouth. She was sunk as a target by the submarines SCEPTRE and SWIFTSURE 14/9/88.

HMS AURIGA

The AURIGA was launched 29/03/45 and completed to the standard A class design with ten torpedo tubes. She was modernised in the 1950s to a streamlined design with just six torpedo tubes (4 bow and 2 stern), originally with a 4 inch gun, (which was later removed) as seen in this photograph. she was part of the Task Group deployed to cover the final stages of the evacuation of Aden. She was sold in 11/74 and broken up at Newport.

HMS AURORA

The Leander class frigate AURORA was completed 9/4/64 by John Brown. She immediately joined the Training Squadron at Portland as the leader. In 1972 she undertook Cod War patrols, and in 9/72 rescued 5 men from an Icelandic fishing boat on fire. She was fitted with the Ikara anti-submarine weapon (1973-6) at Chatham. In 1986 she escorted the Royal Yacht in the Mediterranean. She paid off 1/5/87 and was sold to Devonport Management Ltd for updating and re-sale but this plan never materialised. She was broken up at Millom arriving 6/9/90.

HMS BACCHANTE

The BACCHANTE was built on the Tyne, completing 5/8/69. In 1970 she served in the NATO Standing Force Atlantic, and the following year stood by in the West Indies during a tense situation in Antigua and Bermuda. In 1976 she undertook Cod War patrols. She was not modernised, and in 1981 returned from Exercise Spring Train in the Middle East destined for reserve. She was sold to the Royal New Zealand Navy however, being renamed WELLINGTON, on 1/10/82.

The BERWICK was a Rothesay class anti-submarine frigate, completed by Harland and Wolff 1/6/61. In 4/66 whilst on Beira patrol her boarding party forced a tanker to turn away from the port. She was modernised at Chatham in 1969-71 with a flight deck aft and new gunnery system. In 11/71 she stood by off St Vincent when a local volcano threatened to erupt. In 1972-3 she undertook Cod War patrols. She was brought forward from the Standby Squadron during the Falklands War, and sent to the West Indies, where she attended the independence celebrations at St Kitts and Nevis in 1983. She paid off 18/10/85, and was towed from Portsmouth for use as a target 18/8/86, being sunk by a Tigerfish torpedo

HMS BILDESTON

The Coastal Minesweeper BILDESTON was the first of her class built being completed 28/4/53 by Doig at Grimsby. She was converted to a minehunter in 1968 and in the early 1980s was part of STANAVFORCHAN. During her refits her appearance changed considerably,with a new bridge, mast and funnel, as well as much minesweeping gear being replaced by minehunting equipment.She completed over 33 years service, paying off 30/11/86. Towed to Bilbao in 8/88 for breaking up.

HMS BIRMINGHAM

The BIRMINGHAM was the second Type 42 destroyer to be built being completed by Cammell Laird at Birkenhead on 12/76. The next year she acted as the Admiralty Board Yacht for the Silver Jubilee Review of the Fleet. She has subsequently been involved in operations in the Persian Gulf, where she escorted 19 million tons of shipping in 6 months, and the Adriatic, where her crew conducted 43 merchant vessel boardings. She had her radars and weapon systems upgraded in 1987 and was refitted again in 1995.

HMS BLACKPOOL

The BLACKPOOL was a Type 12 frigate, built by Harland and Wolff completing 12/8/58. After several commissions in the Far East, she was lent to the Royal New Zealand Navy from 6/66-71. On return she was laid up awaiting disposal, and was eventually used for underwater explosive trials at Rosyth (with her turret replaced by a mast) before being broken up 5/78.

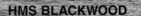

HMS BLACKWOOD

The BLACKWOOD was a Type 14 frigate, completed by Thornycroft 22/8/57. She was used as a submarine target ship and then worked in the Second Training Squadron at Portland and later as leader of the Fishery Protection Squadron. She suffered serious hull damage from ice and became a harbour training ship at Portsmouth, then an accommodation ship at Rosyth before returning as a training ship at Portsmouth 1970-74. She was broken up at Troon 16/11/76.

HMS BLAKE

The cruiser BLAKE was the last of the Tiger Class, and hence the last RN cruiser, to be completed. Built by Fairfields, she commissioned in 03/61, 19 years after being laid down. She had two twin 6 inch automatic turrets, but 4 years later started a refit at Portsmouth, losing her after turret and being fitted with a hangar and flight deck. The refit completed in 1969, and she emerged with an ungainly appearance. She retained her forward 6 inch turret and twin 3 inch guns, but her after 3 inch guns were replaced by Seacat mountings. She paid off in 1979 and arrived at Cairnryan to be broken up in 10/82.

HMS BRIGHTON

The BRIGHTON was a Rothesay class frigate, completed by Yarrow 28/9/61. She was off Aden during a show of force in 5/67, and was the first Gibraltar guardship in 10/67. She completed a modernisation at Chatham in 11/71, during which she was fitted with a flight deck aft. In 1974 she was part of the force that evacuated British nationals from Cyprus following the Turkish invasion. The next year she undertook Cod War patrols. She arrived on the Medway 16/9/85 to be broken up.

HMS BRISTOL

The BRISTOL was the only Type 82 destroyer built - completed by Swan Hunter in 12/72. Designed to operate with aircraft carriers that were never built, she was unusual with her three funnels. Having a large hull she was used for weapon trials and in 11/86 fired her 50th Seadart missile - the RN's 500th. She took part in the Falklands War, and was in the Dartmouth Training Squadron prior to paying off in 06/91. She then relieved the KENT as a Harbour Training Ship at Portsmouth.

HMS BROADSWORD

The BROADSWORD was the first RN warship to be specified and built in metric units and to have an all missile armament. She was built by Yarrow, being launched 12/5/76 and accepted 21/2/79. At 3,556 tons and with a length of 430 feet, her Olympus gas turbine engines could drive her at 30 knots, whilst she could cruise on her Tyne gas turbines at 18. In 1980 she aided the Fastnet Race yachts caught in bad weather. Her involvement in the Falklands War, during which she suffered bomb damage and rescued 170 of COVENTRY's, crew, led to her being fitted with light AA guns. In 1995 she recovered smuggled drums of cocaine from the sea in the West Indies. She paid off 31/3/95 and transferred to Brazil as the FREGATA GREENHALGH 30/6/95.

HMS BRONINGTON

The BRONINGTON was completed 4/6/54 by Cook, Welton and Gemmell, and was immediately renamed HUMBER and served with the RNR until the Humber Division of the Reserve was disbanded 4 years later. She was converted to a minehunter in 1965, and was commanded by HRH Prince Charles from 2/76. She also carried out patrols off Northern Ireland and served in the Fishery Protection Squadron. Paid off 30.6.88. In 1989 she was towed to Manchester where she has since been opened as a Museum Ship.

HMS BUCKLESHAM

The BUCKLESHAM was an inshore minesweeper, but is photographed here having been converted for Port Auxiliary Service at Portland, with her 20mm gun removed and an enclosed bridge fitted. She had been completed at Ardrossan in 1954 and then placed in reserve, which included 5 years on land cradles. In 1965 she was brought forward and re-fitted as a torpedo recovery vessel. She was sold to Pounds at Portsmouth in 3/81.

HMS BULWARK

Laid down just before the end of World War II the BULWARK was completed by Harland and Wolff at Belfast in 11/54. She took part in the Suez campaign as an aircraft carrier, and in 1959-60 was converted to a Commando Carrier at Portsmouth. She was the first of her type, operating helicopters in support of ship-borne Commando, and served for long periods in the Far East, and later was headquarters ship for the British withdrawal from Malta. In her modified role she also carried out exercises as an anti-submarine helicopter carrier in the late 70s. She finally paid off in 03/81 after long and valuable service - being known affectionately as "The Rusty B" - and was towed to Cairnryan for breaking up in 04/84.

HMS CAPRICE

The CAPRICE was one of the last group of Emergency War design destroyers, completing in 04/44 and serving on Arctic convoys before joining the British Pacific Fleet. Paid off in 1946, ten years later she was modernised with a new fire control system, bridge and with Squid aft. She then served in the Far East, and in 1963 was guardship in British Guyana during a long General strike there. In 1971 she relieved MANXMAN as Training Ship for the RNEC Manadon, and patrolled off Iceland during the 1973 Cod War. She was towed to Queenborough in 10/79 for breaking up.

HMS CARDIFF

The CARDIFF was launched by Vickers at Barrow in 1974 but was completed, by Swan Hunter, in 1979, work having been suspended on her in 06/75 to allow the yard to concentrate on the Argentinian destroyer HERCULES. She was returning from the Straits of Hormuz when the Falklands War started, and headed south instead of north from Gibraltar. She used her Sea Dart against a shadowing aircraft and also at C-130s trying to resupply the islands. She was refitted at Portsmouth in 1988, when new air search radar was installed. Later she served in the Gulf War where her helicopter destroyed Iraqi patrol boats. She carried out West Indies Guardship duties, being at the Columbus 500 celebrations in the Bahamas and also assisting in hurricane relief operations in 1992.

HMS CAVALIER

CAVALIER was completed by Samuel White at Cowes in 11/44 and took part in operations off Norway and Arctic convoys. Joined the East Indies Station just after the war had ended, and was engaged in operations off Java. She was placed in reserve in 1946, and was modernised in 1955-57, joining the Far East Fleet. She carried out guard duties off Gan, and was involved in early actions in Brunei in 1962. Later she undertook Beira patrols and guardship duties at Gibraltar. She paid off in 1972, was sold to the CAVALIER Trust in 10/77 and has since been on display at Southampton and Brighton and then laid up at Hebburn. In 1998 was destined to be moved again and opened to the public.

HMS CHARYBDIS

The CHARYBDIS, known as the CHERRY-B, was a Leander class frigate built by Harland and Wolff and completed 15/7/69. She was present at the Western Fleet Review in Torbay . She undertook Cod War patrols in 1973. Modernised with Exocet 1980-2. She was prepared for disposal in 1991, and used as a target, being towed out to be sunk 11/6/93.

HMS CHURCHILL

The CHURCHILL was the Navy's fourth nuclear Fleet submarine, and was completed by Vickers-Armstrong at Barrow 15/07/70. Of 4,400 tons, with a dived displacement of 4,900, she was considered very large by contemporary standards. She was armed with six torpedo tubes. She took part in the Jubilee Review at Spithead in 1977, with the Captain 3rd Submarine Squadron embarked. She paid off 28/02/91.

HMS CLEOPATRA

The CLEOPATRA was built in Devonport Dockyard, being completed 1/3/66. In 1973 she was one of the first frigates in Icelandic waters when the Cod War broke out. She was modified with Exocet in 1973-5 and was the first Leander fitted with towed array sonar in 1982. She paid off at Devonport 6/1/92 and was laid up and de-equipped at Portsmouth. She was sold for breaking up, leaving Portsmouth under tow 21/9/93 for Alang. The tow parted off South Africa, but she was eventually recovered and she arrived to be beached 31/1/94.

CONFIANCE

The CONFIANCE was completed in 1956 by A & J Inglis, one of a class of five Ocean tugs with twin controllable pitch propellers driven by Paxman diesels - giving a speed of 13 knots. She had a range of 5,000 miles at that speed. She was based at Portsmouth, with a spell at Malta from 1957 to 1960. Finally allocated to Devonport in 1966. She was expended as a target 25/7/84.

HMS CONQUEROR

The CONQUEROR was the fifth RN nuclear fleet submarine to be built and was completed 9/11/71 by Cammell Laird. She became the first nuclear submarine to fire a shot in anger when she sank the Argentinian cruiser BELGRANO in May 1982 during the Falklands War. Fitted with Sub Harpoon in 1985, she was in collision with a yacht off the Mull of Kintyre 07/88, she paid off 2/8/90 and laid up at Devonport with her reactor core removed.

HMS COURAGEOUS

The COURAGEOUS was the last of her class, completed 16/10/72 at Barrow. She had a single screw and her engines developed 15,000 shaft horse power giving her an underwater speed of about 30 knots. She took part in the Falklands War. She paid off 10/4/92 and was laid up at Devonport with her reactor core removed.

HMS COVENTRY

The third of the Type 42 destroyers, COVENTRY was completed by Cammell Laird in 10/78. The early ships were completed with Type 965 "double bedstead" radar, and the class carried Sea Dart AA missiles, making them capable of operating as early warning ships. The COVENTRY was one of the first group of ships involved in the Falklands War, and was sunk when hit by 3 bombs in a concerted air attack on 25/5/82. 19 of her crew lost their lives.

HMS CUXTON

The coastal minesweeper CUXTON was one of the first of her class, being completed in 1954. She spent her first 21 years in reserve, including 7 years at Gibraltar, eventually commissioning into the 1st MCMS in 1975. She served on Fishery Protection duties and with the Tay Division of the RNR. In 1987 she patrolled off Blackpool supporting the policing of the Conservative Party Conference. She paid off 23/3/91 and was towed to Bruges for breaking up 16/4/92.

HMS DIAMOND

The DIAMOND was completed in 02/52, one of the last class of traditional destroyers, powerfully armed with three twin 4.5 inch guns and ten torpedo tubes, with a speed of 34 knots. She was damaged in 1953 in a collision with the cruiser SWIFTSURE. In 1956 she took part in the Suez operations. Later modernised with a reduced torpedo tube armament and improved gunnery fire control system, she still retained her graceful but formidable looks. She became a Harbour Training Ship at Portsmouth in 1970, and survived through the 1970s, before being towed to the Medway for breaking up in 11/81.

HMS DIDO

The DIDO was a Leander class frigate built by Yarrow, completing 13/9/63. She was originally to have been the Rothesay class frigate HASTINGS. In 1/66 she put an armed party onboard a merchant ship in the Arabian Sea when the master had difficulty with his crew. She was fitted with an Ikara missile in place of her gun turret 1975-78. She was sold to New Zealand, being renamed SOUTHLAND on 18/7/83, sailing after a refit at Southampton. She was paid off in 1995.

HMS DITTISHAM

The DITTISHAM was an inshore minesweeper built by Fairlie in 1954. She was placed in reserve, but in 1968 became a training tender to HMS GANGES at Shotley, transferring to HMS RALEIGH at Torpoint in 1973, hence this photograph showing a large trainee crew, instead of the usual 15, as she sails out of Devonport. She was sold 3/83 and became TS STEADFAST for the Kingston Sea Cadets, finally being towed to Pounds at Portsmouth 4/97 for scrap.

HMS DREADNOUGHT

The DREADNOUGHT was launched on Trafalgar Day 1960 and completed 17/4/63. The first RN nuclear submarine, she displaced 3,000 tons - small by modern standards. The success of her design led to further construction. She visited the North Pole in 1971. In 1977 she took part in the Jubilee Review and later that year was deployed to the South Atlantic when the Argentinians laid claim to the Falklands and tensions mounted. She was finally laid up in 1982 at Chatham and then towed to Rosyth 13/4/83.

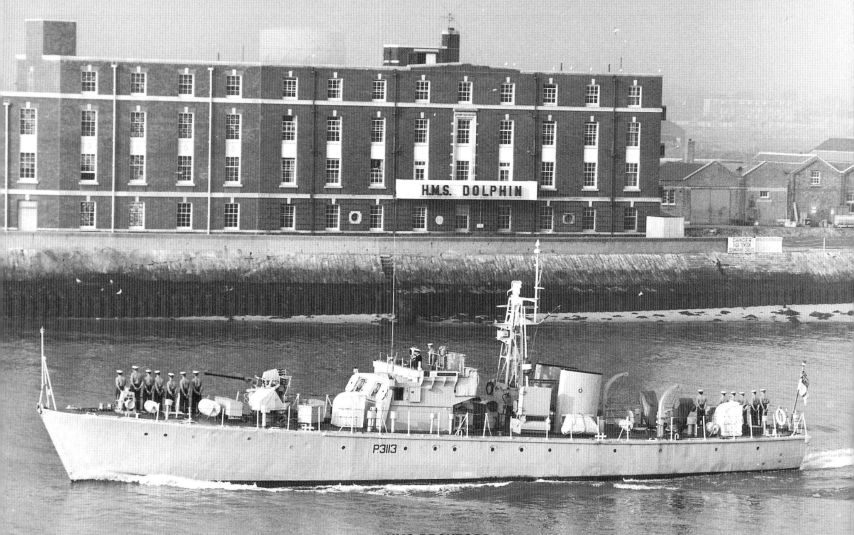

HMS DROXFORD

The DROXFORD was one of a large class of Seaward Defence boats built in the 1950s. At 120 tons, armed with a single 40 mm gun, her diesel engines could drive her at 18 knots. She was built at Northwich and launched 28/1/54. Renamed DEE from 1955-65 whilst attached to the RNR, she was later used by the RN Unit of Glasgow and Strathclyde University. She was for sale in 1984, but was in use as a target boat based at Milford Haven by 1989.

HMS DUNDAS

The DUNDAS was a Type 14 anti-submarine frigate, completed by Samuel White 16/3/56. She was the first anti-submarine frigate laid down after the war. Built in prefabricated sections, this class were found wanting in hull strength in heavy seas, and had to have their hulls strengthened. She spent most of her active career as a training ship in the waters around Portland, though in 10/58 she visited Arctic waters on Fishery protection duties, and again in 1976 she undertook Cod War patrols off Iceland. She paid off in 1978 and was sold 30/11/82 to be broken up at Troon.

HMS EAGLE

The EAGLE was completed in 10/51, 4 years before her more famous sister (ARK ROYAL). Her appearance was altered considerably during her refit in 1959-64, when type 984 radar was fitted on her island structure, with a double bedstead Type 965 radar abaft it replacing the original tripod mast and smaller radars. Her guns were removed to allow room for extra crew to support the ever increasingly complex and sophisticated aircraft borne. She served world-wide, and finally returned from the Far East in late 1971 and paid off in early 1972, lying in the River Tamar for many years until towed to Cairnryan in 10/78 to be broken up.

HMS EASTBOURNE

The EASTBOURNE was a Type 12 frigate, launched by Vickers-Armstrongs Barrow, and completed 9/1/58 on the Tyne. The only one of the first 6 ships to be fitted with stabilisers, she was modified with extra boats and deckhouses aft for service in the Dartmouth Training Squadron 1962-64. She took part in Cod War patrols in 1976 and was in collision with the Icelandic gunboat BALDUR on 22/5/76. She was used for harbour training duties at Rosyth from 1978, until being broken up at Inverkeithing 7/3/85.

RFA ENGADINE

The ENGADINE was built specially as a Helicopter Support Ship by Robb at Leith and completed 12/67. With a speed of 16 knots, she could carry 4 Wessex and 2 Wasp helicopters, or 2 Seakings, and provided training for anti-submarine helicopter crews in deep water. In 1969 the first deck landing by a Westland Wessex took place onboard. In 1976 she stood by off Lebanon ready to evacuate British nationals. She was at the 1977 Jubilee Review and served during the Falklands War. She paid off in 1989 at Devonport and was sold to the Dido Shipping Company, towed to Greece in 2/90 but later resold to Indian shipbreakers arriving at Alang 7/5/96.

HMS ENTERPRISE

ENTERPRISE was one of three E Class Inshore Survey Craft, and was built by M W Blackmore and Sons Ltd at Bideford. She was built for coastal and harbour hydrographic survey operations and had two echo sounding machines and sonar for wreck location. She also carried modern radar, wire sweep gear and an echo sounding launch. ENTERPRISE was sold to the Marine Society in 1986 for use as a source of spares for her sister ECHO, which was also sold - and renamed EARL OF ROMNEY.

HMS EXMOUTH

The EXMOUTH was a Type 14 frigate built by Samuel White and completed 20/12/57. She became a submarine target ship after a period in reserve. She was converted to a gas turbine trials ship in 1966-68 at Chatham, fitted with one Olympus and 2 Proteus engines, giving her a speed of 28 knots. In early 1976 she undertook Cod War patrols, and shortly afterwards stood by to evacuate British Nationals from the Lebanon. She was towed for breaking up at Briton Ferry 3/2/79.

HMS FALMOUTH

The FALMOUTH was a Rothesay Class frigate completed by Swan Hunter 25/7/61. She was modernised at Portsmouth completing 2/71. In 11/75 she was the first RN ship on patrol when Iceland extended its territorial waters to 200 miles. On 6/5/76 she had three collisions with the Icelandic gunboat TYR and had to retire with serious damage. She was brought forward from Standby Squadron during the Falklands War, and carried out South Atlantic patrols. She became a harbour training ship at Portsmouth from 1984-88. Towed to Spain for breaking up 4/5/89.

HMS FAWN

The Coastal Survey Ship FAWN was built at Lowestoft, completing in 1968. The class were built to commercial standards, with a passive tank stabiliser system to reduce rolling and were fitted with the most modern echo sounders and precision radar. She had 4 diesel engines driving 2 shafts giving a speed of 15 knots on controllable pitch propellers. She became non operational in 09/91 and was sold to German interests as an oil exploration vessel, being renamed RED FULMAR to operate off West Africa and in the China Sea.

HMS FEARLESS

The Assault Ship FEARLESS was built by Harland and Wolff at Belfast, and was completed in 11/65. Basically designed to transport troops and equipment and land them using landing craft accessing the ship through her stern ramp, she can also operate in a heliborne assault role. For self defence she was fitted with Seacat missiles and Bofors guns. In 1990 she was fitted with Vulcan Phalanx and 20 mm B Marc guns. She operated in the Far East, was used for the Rhodesian/UK talks at Gibraltar in 1968, and played a significant part in the Falklands War. Afterwards she was a Dartmouth Training Ship prior to paying off in 1985. However she recommissioned in 1990 and is scheduled to run on until the new LPDRs are completed, early in the next century.

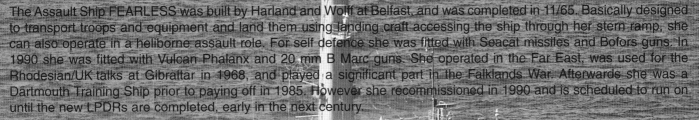

HMS FIFE

The FIFE was a County class guided missile destroyer, completed by Fairfield in 06/66 . She was built with the improved Seaslug missile system, and later had a gun turret replaced by Exocet launchers. She suffered a major fire in 11/70. In 08/79 she went to the aid of Dominica after a hurricane had struck the area, and was awarded the Sword of Peace for her work. For her last year of service she was in the Dartmouth Training Squadron, paying off after being used as a Floating Trade Centre in Canada in 06/87. She was the last RN warship to use hammocks regularly. She was sold to Chile in 07/87 and renamed BLANCO ENCALADA.

HMS GALATEA

The Leander class frigate GALATEA was completed 25/4/64 by Swan Hunter. She was fitted with an Ikara missile system 1971-74 at Devonport. She undertook Cod War patrols 1975-76, being in collision with the Icelandic gunboat BALDUR 26/3/76. In 1977 became the first ship to use the new frigate complex at Devonport. She paid off in 1986 and was towed from Portsmouth 13/6/88 for use as a target, being sunk on 22/6/88.

HMS GLASSERTON

The GLASSERTON was a Ton Class coastal minesweeper, built by Doig in 1954. She was fitted with Osbourne mine destroyer unit. In the 1970s she was employed on patrols off Northern Ireland. She joined the London Division RNR in 1979, becoming a static training ship by 1983. She was so employed until sold and towed from the Thames 8/12/87 for Pounds at Portsmouth. She was then resold for breaking up in Spain.

RFA GOLD ROVER

The GOLD ROVER is a 7570 ton (gross) Fleet Tanker, built by Swan Hunter completing in 1974. Diesel driven, she is capable of 19 knots and had a flight deck abaft the funnel for vertrep operations. She can carry a limited range of dry and refrigerated stores as well as fuel warships supplied either abeam or astern. She temporarily flew the flag of FO 2nd Flotilla in the Pacific in 1975 during a deployment during which she visited 60 ports. She carried the Commodore of the RFA at the Jubilee Review in 1977. In 1986 she aided Jamaica during flood relief operations.

HMS GRENVILLE

The GRENVILLE was built as the Leader of the U class of emergency war design destroyers, completing in 05/43, serving in the Channel then the Mediterranean at Anzio, and returning to the Channel for D Day before joining the British Pacific Fleet. She was converted to a frigate in 1953/4 and served in the Portland Training Squadron. After a period in reserve, she became a trials ship for ASWE, being fitted with a new bridge and enclosed foremast. She was laid up in 1974 and broken up, at Queenborough, in 02/83.

HMS AVENGER

The AVENGER was the last of the Type 21 frigates built. She was completed by Yarrow 15/4/78 and served in the Falklands War, firing well over 1000 rounds of 4.5 inch shells in coastal bombardments. Remained after the War had been won and transferred 900 prisoners from West Falklands to Port Stanley. In 11/93 she assisted in the arrest of the drug smuggling ship POSEIDEN. She paid off 23/9/94 and was sold to Pakistan and became the TIPPU SULTAN.

HMY BRITANNIA

The Royal Yacht BRITANNIA was built on the Clyde and first commissioned in 01/54. With graceful lines and a speed of 22 knots, she travelled the world extensively, and in 1986 assisted in the evacuation of civilians from the Yemen. Her final overseas voyage was to Hong Kong to bring back the departing Governor in 1997. She then undertook a tour around Britain before paying off at Portsmouth, amid controversy about her possible replacement and her future. It is, perhaps, a trifle sad - if not symbolic - that she was completed just too late for the Coronation Fleet Review, and paid off before the Golden Jubilee Review. Moved to Edinburgh 1998 to be opened to the public.

HMS CUTLASS

The CUTLASS was a Fast Training Boat built by Vosper Thornycroft in 1970. Powered by two Proteus gas turbines, with diesels for cruising, she used her 40 knot speed to exercise the Fleet in tactics against fast surface targets. She was sold to a private Greek buyer in 2/83.

HMS CYGNET

The CYGNET was a Bird Class Patrol Boat of 190 tons. She was built on the Humber in 1975/6. She was driven by 2 diesels at 21 knots. She was armed with a 40mm gun, mounted on her stern, as seen in this photograph. In 1981/83 she assisted in patrolling the coast of Northern Ireland to deter the smuggling of arms and personnel. She was sold to a private individual at Southampton in 02/96.

HMS DIOMEDE

The DIOMEDE was one of the last Leander class frigates built for the Royal Navy, the last class with steam propulsion. She was completed by Yarrow 16/10/70. She retained her gun turret throughout her career. On 1/11/71 she went to the aid of the Liberian tanker ESPIA on fire in the English Channel, bringing the fire under control. On three occasions in early 1976 she was in collision with the Icelandic gunboats BALDUR and TYR during the Cod War. She paid off 31/5/88 and was sold to Pakistan 13/7/88 being renamed SHAMSHER.

HMS ENDURANCE

Built in Denmark in 1956/7. the ANITA DAN was renamed ENDURANCE and became the Royal Navy's Ice Patrol Ship, being converted by Harland and Wolff in 1967/8. She had regular, seasonal patrols in the South Atlantic, and was about to be withdrawn permanently when the Falklands War broke out. She took a major role in the opening moves of that war. Known as the "Red Plum" because of the colour of her hull, she had several incidents in the ice, running aground in 03/84, when she was towed off by the research ship BRANSFIELD, and being holed in 02/89, later undergoing repairs at Deception Island. She paid off in 11/91 and was sold to London based Pakistani interests, arriving at Karachi in 01/93.

HMS FLINTHAM

The Inshore Minesweeper FLINTHAM was built by Bolson, completing on 1/11/55. Placed in reserve for her first 9 years, she then became a training tender, first to HMS GANGES at Shotley, and then to HMS RALEIGH at Torpoint, giving many young sailors their first taste of life at sea. In this role, indicated by the badge on her mast, she attended the Jubilee Review at Spithead. She was sold in 1983.

HMS FOX

FOX, like her three sisters, was built by Brooke Marine at Lowestoft, and could carry a 28.5 foot survey launch on her davits. At 800 tons, with a crew of 38, this class were replacements for the coastal minesweeper conversions for coastal survey operations. The class were air conditioned throughout. HRH Prince Charles served in her briefly in 1973. She became non-operational in 12/88 and was towed to Portsmouth in 02/89 prior to being sold to commercial interests in 04/89.

HMS GLASGOW

The GLASGOW was launched by Swan Hunter in 04/76 and was completed in 03/79, the fifth and last of the Type 42 destroyers to be completed in the 70s. During the Falklands War she was hit in the engine room by a 1000lb bomb, which fortunately did not explode, but caused so much damage that she had to limp back to the United Kingdom after emergency repairs. Subsequently refitted with improved close range weapons and new radar, she has served in the Mediterranean Standing Force, the Adriatic and Gulf, where she operated with the Russian destroyer ADMIRAL VINOGRADOV in 02/94.

HMS HERALD

The first three H class Ocean Survey Ships built in the mid 1960s were so successful that a fourth, the slightly larger HERALD, was built by Robb Caledon at Leith, completing in 10/74. Her single screw, propelled by a diesel electric engine gives her a speed of 14 knots, with a 20,000 mile endurance at 9 knots. In the late 1970s she carried out survey work in the Indian Ocean. In the 1982 Falklands War she was used as a Hospital Ship in the South Atlantic, and was painted grey in 1983/4 as an MCM depot ship. In 1988 she relieved the ABDIEL as MCMV Depot ship in the Persian Gulf, being fitted with two 20mm guns. In the '90s she was employed on survey duties in the South Atlantic.

HMS JUPITER

The Leander class frigate JUPITER is pictured here at Venice. She was built by Yarrow, completing 24/6/69 as one of the last group of Leander class frigates, fitted with Y160 machinery. She stood by during unrest ashore in Trinidad in 1970, and again off St Lucia in 1972. In 1973 she took part in the Cod War patrols. She was fitted with Seawolf and Exocet missiles in 1981/82. In 1986 she was one of the ships which evacuated refugees from South Yemen. In 1990-1 she was involved in the Gulf War. She was sold for breaking up in India 9/97.

HMS KIRKLISTON

The KIRKLISTON was one of the large number of Ton Class coastal minesweepers built for the Royal and other Navies. Completed 21/8/54 by Harland and Wolff, she became the RNR KILMOREY on commissioning. In 1964 she was converted to a Minehunter, being fitted with an active rudder for slow speed manoeuvring. She then served at Hong Kong till 1972. In 1974 she became the first minehunter manned by the RNR. She was one of a Squadron deployed to the Gulf of Suez in 1984 to search for mines. She was placed in the Stand By Squadron in 1987 and in 10/91 was towed to Bruges for breaking up.

HMS OSIRIS

The OSIRIS was completed by Vickers-Armstrongs 11/1/64. A diesel electric submarine based on a successful design, she completed 28 years service, running 500,000 miles of which 160,000 were submerged. She paid off 05/92 and was sold to the Canadian government and was dismantled for spares. Her engines were later fitted in her Canadian sister OJIBWA.

HMS SHEFFIELD

The SHEFFIELD was the lead ship of the Type 42 class of destroyers, being built by Vickers at Barrow and accepted in 02/75. She had distinctive "muffs" on her funnels. The class were the first all gas turbine propelled destroyers in the Royal Navy. SHEFFIELD was one of the first ships involved in the Falklands War, and was hit by an Exocet missile on 04/05/82. She was abandoned and finally sank on 10 May whilst under tow.

HMS SOVEREIGN

The SOVEREIGN was the second S class nuclear fleet submarine, a very successful design developed from the first nuclear submarines. She was completed by Vickers-Armstrongs on 11/07/77, having been launched by Lady Ashmore 17/02/73. With a crew of 97, these vessels are capable of world wide deployments and can maintain high speeds whilst remaining silent. SOVEREIGN visited the North Pole in 1976. She has undergone refits and the upgrading of her communications and weapons fits, and underwent a four year refit at Rosyth before being recommissioned in 1996.

HMS WOODLARK

The WOODLARK was built as the Inshore Minesweeper YAXHAM. She was launched by Samuel White in 01/58, and in 1964 was converted along the lines of the E Class Survey craft for inshore survey work in Home Waters, and renamed. In 10/78 she assisted with the oil pollution clearance operation when a Greek tanker ran aground off Milford Haven. She continued survey work till 1980, when she became a tender to Southampton University RN Unit. In 1986 she was towed to Milford Haven to be used as a target.

GRIPER

The GRIPER was a Director Class Fleet servicing tug, with diesel engines driving paddle wheels electrically. The propulsion system gave a rapid response. Her mast could be lowered for working under the overhang of aircraft carriers, as can be seen in this photograph. Built by Wm Simons at Renfrew in 1958, she served at Rosyth and Portsmouth before being sold on 6/12/79 to Pounds at Portsmouth. She was broken up in Spain in 1980.

HMS GURKHA

The general purpose frigate GURKHA was completed by Thornycroft 13/2/63. In 1966 she stood by with an Army company embarked during an oil dispute in the Persian Gulf. During the Indo-Pakistan war in 1971 she stood by to evacuate British nationals from the area. In 1973-76 she carried out Cod War patrols, and was in four collisions with the Icelandic gunboat ODINN on 6/5/76, and three the following day, having to retire with serious damage. Paid off to the Standby Squadron in 7/80, she was brought forward and refitted during the Falklands War, replacing a vessel sunk. In 4/84 she was sold to Indonesia, refitted at Southampton sailed as WILHEMOS ZAKARIAS YOHANNES.

HMS HARDY

The HARDY was the first Type 14 frigate built, completed on 8/12/55, by Yarrow. The after 40mm gun in these ships was removed early in their careers due to hull strengthening problems. Serving mainly in the Londonderry and Portland areas, she paid off to the Standby Squadron 8/77, then, after another short spell operational service at Portland, became a stores and accommodation ship in Portsmouth 10/79. She was used as a target for Exocet missiles and was finally sunk, by torpedo, in the Western Approaches 3/7/84.

HARDY

F54

HMS HARTLAND POINT

One of many maintenance ships built in Canada towards the end of World War II on standard merchant ship lines, HARTLAND POINT was one of three to survive into the 1970s in the Royal Navy. She was modernised in 1959/60 and served in the Far East as an Escort Maintenance Ship from 1960-65, when she was relieved by TRIUMPH and returned to the United Kingdom, where she spent a period in reserve. In 1972-73 she was used as an accommodation ship in Belfast, until, in 07/74, was sold to the Marine Oil Industry for use as an oil rig repair vessel. She was finally broken up at Santander in 1979.

RFA HEBE

The HEBE was a stores Carrier, built in 1962 by Henry Robb, she displaced 4823 tons (gross) and had a speed of 15 knots. On completion, she was chartered from BISN Co to carry dry and refrigerated cargo as well as lub oil and water. In 1964 she helped evacuate British nationals from Zanzibar. In 1976 she towed the damaged CHERRYLEAF across the Indian Ocean. She herself was damaged by fire in 1976 in Gibraltar. Her charter was terminated that year and she became the Greek MV GOOD GUARDIAN.

HMS HECATE

The HECATE was completed in 12/65. Her main duties during the 70's were surveys in North Atlantic and Home waters. She had a bomb attached to her hull whilst on a visit to Nantes, but it failed to explode and in 1980 two of her survey launches were damaged by IRA bombs. In 1981 she suffered damage from a freak wave when water entered through her funnel. She was refitting during the Falklands War, but completed, in grey livery, to relieve the ENDURANCE on patrol. She carried out further survey work in the North Atlantic before her disposal, which had been delayed because of the Gulf War. She was sold in 12/93 sailing from Portsmouth to India to be broken up.

HMS HERMES

Built as an aircraft carrier, being laid down at Barrow in 1944 but not completed until 10/50, she emerged as a larger, very distinct version of her sisters, and was fitted with 984 radar. She served, mainly in the Far East, as an aircraft carrier, but in 03/71 was taken in hand for conversion to a Commando carrier, completing in 1973. Three years later she was again converted, this time with a primary anti-submarine helicopter role, whilst still retaining her Commando capability. In 1980 was modified with a ramp forward as a Sea Harrier strike carrier. In this guise she was the Flagship of the Task Force in the Falklands War. She was sold to the Indian Navy in 04/86, and handed over in 05/87 after a refit at Devonport, being renamed VEERAT.

HMS HUBBERSTON

The HUBBERSTON was built as a Ton class minesweeper at Gosport completing 14/10/55. After 5 years in reserve, she was converted to a minehunter at Chatham, and served in the Far East for 7 years. In 1975 she took part in the second Suez Canal clearance operation. She was refitted 30 years later to extend her life as a minehunter. She paid off at Portsmouth 21/2/91 and was towed to Belgium 13/5/92 for breaking up.

HMS HYDRA

The third of three H class Ocean Survey ships built for the Royal Navy by Yarrow in the 1960s, she was completed in 05/66. This class were the first designed with a combined oceanographical and hydrographical role. They were built to merchant ship design with good accommodation and endurance. HYDRA entered the 1970's in the Far East, surveying around Malacca and Singapore, and later, carried out surveys in the South West Pacific before returning to the United Kingdom for a refit in 1976/7. In 1982 she was employed as a hospital ship during the Falklands War. In 1986 assisted the evacuation of civilians from the Yemen. She was sold to the Indonesian Navy on 18/04/86 and renamed DEWA KEMBAR.

HMS INTREPID

The second of the assault ships built, INTREPID was completed in 03/67. In 1972 she was used as a Dartmouth Training Ship, and in 1982 took part in the Falklands War, a role for which she was ideally suited. Refitted in 1985 at a cost of £28 million with improved communications and extra close range AA weapons. Laid up at Portsmouth since 1990, she has been in a state of preservation, with short docking periods to keep her nominally available until the new LPDRs are completed.

HMS ISIS

The ISIS was built as the Ley Class inshore minehunter CRADLEY. The Ley Class could be distinguished from the Ham class minesweepers by their extended deckhouse and lack of sweeping gear. They also had smaller engines as they were not required to tow sweep gear. She was launched in 1955 by Saunders Roe, and maintained in reserve until she was renamed in 1963, when allocated to the London Division RNR. Later she was attached to the Southampton University RN Unit. She was sold in 1/82 to Pounds at Portsmouth for further use.

HMS IVESTON

The IVESTON was built at Dartmouth, completing 6/55. She was then placed in reserve before being converted to a minehunter in 1963-4. In 5/78 she assisted with the oil clearance operation when the Greek tanker ELENE V was cut in two by another vessel in the North Sea. She carried out patrols off Northern Ireland in the 1980s, and was given a life extension refit 1983-4. She paid off 21/7/92, was placed in reserve, but then loaned to the Sea Cadets at Thurrock in 8/93.

M1151

HMS JAGUAR

The JAGUAR was a Type 41, anti-aircraft frigate. She was built by Denny, completing 12/12/59 - the last warship built by that company. These ships were diesel driven, capable of 25 knots and with a long endurance. Heavily armed with two twin 4.5 inch gun turrets, a twin 40mm gun and squid, they were later given seacat missiles. By the time of this photograph her after "mack" had been plated over, and she carried a single 40 mm gun abaft it. In 1973 she took part in Cod War patrols, being in collision with the Icelandic gunboat THOR 10/9/73. She was sold to Bangladesh 6/7/78 and renamed ALI HAIDER.

HMS JERSEY

The JERSEY was the first of the Island class Offshore Protection Vessels, built by Hall Russell at Aberdeen and launched by the Princess Royal 18/3/76. At 925 tons, she was fitted with a single screw propelled by a diesel engine giving her 16.5 knots, with a range of 7,000 miles. Built on trawler lines to protect North Sea Oil installations and undertake fishery patrols. She was sold to Bangladesh on 28/1/94 and renamed SHAHEED RAHUL AMIN.

HMS JUNO

The Leander class frigate JUNO was completed 18/7/67 by Thornycroft. In 1972 and 1976 she undertook Cod War patrols, being in two collisions with the Icelandic gunboat THOR on 6/2/76, and three with the TYR on 12/3/76. She took part in the BBC TV series as HMS HERO. In 1981-4 she was converted to a navigational training ship at Rosyth, with her weapons and directors removed. She paid off 4/12/92 and was towed to Vigo for breaking up 8/2/95.

HMS KENT

The KENT was one of the first County class guided missile destroyers, armed with four 4.5 inch guns and the early Seaslug missile system, she was completed in 08/63. She carried out patrols in the Far East during confrontation with Indonesia, and in 1968 was a host ship for talks over the future of Southern Rhodesia - at Gibraltar. Latterly she served in Home Waters, and was Flagship for a visit to Sweden in 1978, when King Carl XVI Gustaf flew his flag onboard in his capacity as an honorary Admiral in the Royal Navy. She paid off 04/80, and became a Harbour Training Ship at Portsmouth until 03/93. She was sold and towed from Portsmouth in 11/97 for breaking up in India.

KINLOSS

The KINLOSS was a coastal salvage vessel built by A Hall of Aberdeen in 1945, and was later designated a Mooring, Salvage and Boom Vessel. She displaced 950 tons and had a speed of 9 knots. Originally steam driven, she had diesel engines fitted in 1963/4. She had a 200 ton lift over the bows. She underwent shock trials at Rosyth in 1988, was sold the next year to be broken up at Inverkeithing.

HMS LALESTON

The LALESTON was launched 18/5/54 by Harland and Wolff, and on completion served in the VERNON squadron. After being placed in reserve in 1964 she was converted to a diving trials ship, commissioning 3/67. Note her open bridge and the decompression chamber aft (in this photograph). In 1977 she joined the Ulster RNR Division. In 1978 she was one of the ships sent to assist the French with the oil pollution disposal operation when the tanker AMOCO CADIZ went aground off Ushant. She paid off in 8/82, and was sold in 12/84 for breaking up.

M1158

HMS LEANDER

The nameship of her class, LEANDER was originally to have been the Rothesay class frigate WEYMOUTH. She was completed by Harland and Wolff 27/3/63. She was converted (at Devonport) to carry Ikara anti-submarine missiles 1971-2. In 1975-6 she took part in Cod War patrols, being in collision with the Icelandic gunboat THOR on 9/1/76 and the VER on 22/5/76, retiring with serious damage after the second collision. On 7/9/82 assisted with firefighting in MV AVE MARIA off North Foreland. She paid off to the Standby Squadron 1986 and was then laid up in Fareham Creek. She was towed from Portsmouth 8/9/89 and expended as a target.

HMS LEOPARD

The LEOPARD was a Type 41 anti-aircraft frigate built at Portsmouth Dockyard and completed 30/12/58. With a good endurance on her 8 diesel engines coupled to two propellers, she served mainly on the South Atlantic Station. In 7/63 she suffered severe damage to her side when in collision with a South African minesweeper during exercises, and she underwent an extended refit when she returned to Portsmouth. She undertook patrols in the Cod War in 1973 and 1975. She paid off 12/75 and was broken up at Dartford 13/10/77.

HMS LINCOLN

The Type 61 aircraft direction frigate LINCOLN was built by Fairfield, completing 7/7/60. This class had the same diesel engine arrangement as the Type 41s, giving them a long endurance. LINCOLN was fitted with 12 ft controllable pitch propellers. Her radar was improved during a refit in 1966-68. She undertook Cod War patrols in 1973, and was in a collision with the gunboat AEGIR 17/7/73 and again (twice) on 22/9/73. After these patrols she had extra wooden strengthening fitted to her bow and stern, as can be seen in this photograph. She was sold 23/3/83 to Thomas Ward and broken up at Inverkeithing.

HMS LLANDAFF

The LLANDAFF was built by Hawthorn Leslie, completing 11/4/58. She was an aircraft direction frigate, and was fitted with long range radar aft. This was modernised in the 1960s, with a double 965 being fitted. She served on the Far East Station for several commissions, where her endurance could be used to good effect. She was sold to Bangladesh 10/12/76 and renamed UMAR FEROOQ.

HMS LONDON

The guided missile destroyer LONDON was completed in 11/63 by Swan Hunter. This class had a combined steam and gas turbine system of propulsion giving them a speed of 32.5 knots. She took part in the evacuation from Aden in 1967. She was Flagship of the First Flotilla at the Silver Jubilee Review in 1977. In 1979 Flag Officer Malta sailed in her from Malta on the final withdrawal. She was sold to Pakistan in 03/82 and renamed BABUR.

HMS LONDONDERRY

The LONDONDERRY was a Rothesay class anti-submarine frigate, built by Samuel White and completed 22/7/60. In 69-70 she was modernised at Rosyth with a flight deck aft. In 1970 she was in the Far East and took part in confrontation with Indonesia and Beira patrols. She became a trials ship in 1979, having been fitted with three masts. Carried out trials of pump-jet propulsion in 1980. Due to pay off in 1982, she was reprieved by the Falklands War and was used as a Dartmouth Training Ship. She became a harbour training ship at Portsmouth 3/84-88 and was sunk as a target 25/6/89.

HMS LOWESTOFT

The LOWESTOFT was a Rothesay class frigate completed 18/10/61 by Stephen. She was the first ship on the Beira patrol in 27/2/66. She was modernised at Chatham 1967-70. On 21/4/72 she went to the aid of a tanker in distress off S Africa. Her crew extinguished a fire onboard before towing it clear of the coast and handing her over to a tug. She undertook patrols in the 1973 Cod War. In 1975 she helped evacuate refugees from Vietnam. She also undertook patrols in the Cod War 1975-6, colliding with the THOR. In her later years (1977-81) she was a sonar trials ship, with equipment housed on her flight deck. In 1982 her flight deck was restored to use when she became Gibraltar guardship. She was sunk as a target by CONQUEROR 8/6/86.

HMS LYNX

The anti-aircraft frigate LYNX was built by John Brown and completed 14/3/57. After three commissions in the South Atlantic, she was the first of the class to be modified, with the after "mack" plated over. She was the last RN ship to be based at Simonstown. She undertook patrols in the 1973 Cod War. Paid off in 7/74, refitted and joined the Standby Squadron. She was sold to Bangladesh 12/3/82 and renamed ABU BAKR.

HMS MAIDSTONE

The MAIDSTONE was built as a submarine depot ship by John Brown, being completed in 05/38. She served in the Mediterranean, at Scapa Flow, and then returned to the Mediterranean before going on to the Indian Ocean, Australia, Subic Bay and Hong Kong. After the war she served in Home waters. Between 1958 and 1962 she was rebuilt at Portsmouth Dockyard, her guns removed and extra equipment added to enable her to support nuclear submarines. She then served six years at Faslane until the new shore base was completed. A refit at Rosyth followed, and she was used as an accommodation ship at Belfast from 1969-1977. She was sold in 05/78 for breaking up.

HMS MANXMAN

The MANXMAN was built as a fast minelayer, completing in 6/41. When built she could steam at 40 knots and carry 160 mines. In 11/42 she was torpedoed and repairs took till 1945 to complete. She then sailed for the Pacific. Post war she assisted with earthquake relief in the Lebanon in 1956, and was involved in the Suez operations the same year. She was converted to support minesweepers (1960-63) with her boiler power reduced, and subsequently served in the Far East. In 1969 she became a training ship for Engineer Officers working out of Devonport. She was sold for breaking up at Newport 1/9/72.

HMS MATAPAN

The MATAPAN was built as a Later Battle Class destroyer, being completed in 09/47. Many of her sisters were never completed, and she spent a long period in reserve at Devonport. It was not until 1969 she was brought forward and converted at Portsmouth as a trials ship. She emerged in 1973 in a hardly recognisable guide - with an extra funnel, enclosed bridge, flight deck aft and newly designed bow, as a sonar trials ships for AUWE. She was sold in 06/79 and broken up at Blyth.

HMS MERMAID

The frigate MERMAID was building at Yarrow's for the Ghana Navy as the BLACK STAR when a coup occurred and the vessel was no longer required - the bill unpaid. She was completed in 1968 and taken over by the Royal Navy in 03/72. Armed with a twin 4 inch gun forward, and a mortar Mk 10 aft, and fitted with a flight deck, she was diesel driven and capable of 24 knots. She spent a period in the Far East and in early 1976 took part in the Cod War off Iceland, being in collisions with the Icelandic gunboats THOR and BALDUR, having to return to UK for repairs after the last incident. In 9/76 she was in collision with the minesweeper FITTLETON, which sank with the loss of 12 men. She was sold to the Royal Malaysian Navy 5/77 and renamed HANG TUAH.

HMS MINERVA

The Leander class frigate MINERVA was completed 14/5/66 on the Tyne. She was in the second group, fitted with Y136 machinery. In 1968-9 she stood by during periods of civil unrest in the West Indies, and in 1975 she took police from Tortola to Grand Turk during further unrest. She was fitted with Exocet missiles in 1978-9, being damaged by a boiler room explosion at Portsmouth 10/78. In 1982 she took part in the Falklands War. In 1991 she was in the Dartmouth Training Squadron. Paid off 30/4/92 having steamed 750,000 miles. She was sold for breaking up and left under tow for India 21/9/93.

HMS MOHAWK

The MOHAWK was a Tribal class general purpose frigate, launched at Barrow and completed on the Tyne 29/11/63. After service in the Persian Gulf, she started a refit in 1970 for service in the Dartmouth Training Squadron. Her after gun was removed to make extra space for boats and her hangar converted to a navigational classroom. The refit was abandoned and reversed and she recommissioned in 1976. In 10/79 she joined the Standby Squadron. She was towed to Cairnryan for breaking up arriving 3/12/82.

HMS NAIAD

The Leander class frigate NAIAD was completed 15/3/65 by Yarrow. She suffered serious damage to her engines when a turbine stripped its blades in 1/72. She then started a refit which lasted to 1975, during which she was fitted with Ikara anti-submarine missiles. She undertook patrols in the Cod War in 1976, and was in collision with the gunboat TYR 24/4/76. She then deployed to the Mediterranean and Indian Ocean. She paid off 1/5/87 and was used as a non seagoing self power generating trials ship. She underwent shock and fire trials in 1988-89, before being towed out to be sunk as a target 28/9/90.

HMS NEWCASTLE

The Type 42 destroyer NEWCASTLE was built, appropriately, by Swan Hunter and commissioned in 03/78. She was refitted in Portsmouth in 1986-7 and the next year was damaged when hit in the engine room by a target she had engaged with her Phalanx CIWS. She carried out South Atlantic patrols, duties as West Indies guardship and took part in Exercise Global 1992, which included visits to Japanese ports.

NEWTON

The NEWTON is a trials vessel for sonar propagation, and was built by Scotts in 1976. She is 2779 tons (gross) and has a speed of 15 knots. She has a limited cable laying capability. In 1977 she was at the Jubilee Review at Spithead. In 7/94 she was damaged by an explosion onboard off the Florida coast. Currently employed by the Defence Research Agency.

HMS NORFOLK

The NORFOLK was one of the last County class destroyers, being launched by Swan Hunter 16/11/67 and completed in 03/70, being fitted with the improved Sea Dart system. In 1974 she carried out trials in the Mediterranean with Exocet missiles fitted in place of her B gun turret. She also carried out periods with STANAVFORLANT in 1972 and 1976. She was sold to Chile in 10/81, being renamed PRAT and sailing from Portsmouth in 1982.

HMS NURTON

The coastal minesweeper NURTON was completed 21/8/57 by Harland and Wolff, and became the RNR training ship MONTROSE till 1960. She was converted to a minehunter in 1965. In 1971 she undertook the first patrol against smugglers running arms into Northern Ireland. She was the RNR KILLIECRANKIE in 1972-3. In 1982 she surveyed the Channel for cable laying operations, and in 1988 undertook the seaward defence of Brighton during the Conservative Party Conference. Paid off 3/12/93, as the last Ton class in commission, having completed 37 years service and covered 326,273 miles. A bid to preserve her failed and she was broken up at Selby 6/95.

HMS OBERON

The OBERON was the first of her class laid down, but was the second completed, being launched on 18/7/59 at Chatham Dockyard by the Duchess of Kent - the first Royal launch there since 1902. A repeat of the successful Porpoise class, they were also purchased by Commonwealth and foreign navies. She paid off 10/12/86. In 2/87 she was purchased by Seaforth Ship Repairers and renamed SEAFORTH A and was taken to Immingham for re-sale. No sale was forthcoming and she was broken up there in 1991.

RFA OLMEDA

The OLMEDA was built as the OLEANDER by Swan Hunter and completed 10/65. Her name was changed in 10/67 to avoid confusion with the frigate LEANDER. One of a class of three fast Fleet Replenishment Ships, larger than the Tide class they replaced and with an extra RAS point. Built with steam turbines for 19 knots but achieving over 21 on trials, she had a hangar and could operate three helicopters. In 1973 she supported the frigates conducting the Cod War. In 1975 she stood by off Cyprus during a period of tension. She took part in the Falklands War in 1982. She sailed from Portsmouth 19/7/94 under her own power for breaking up in India.

HMS OLYMPUS

OLYMPUS was built at Barrow and was completed 7/7/62. She was damaged in a berthing collision with the TRAFALGAR at Faslane in 3/89. Later she damaged her fin, and it was replaced using the fin from the Porpoise class submarine CACHALOT - she became known as IMPALOT. She paid off 28/7/89 and sailed to Halifax where she became a Harbour Training Ship for the Canadian Navy.

HMS OTTER

The OTTER was built by Scotts, and was completed 20/8/62. This class were fitted with 8 torpedo tubes, (6 bow and 2 stern) and could carry 30 torpedoes. They had a speed of 17 knots submerged and 12 knots on the surface, using diesel electric propulsion. She paid off 31/7/91 and was sold in 1992 and broken up at Portsmouth.

HMS PHOEBE

The Leander class frigate PHOEBE was completed by Stephen 8/7/66. She was part of the task force assembled for the withdrawal from Aden. In 12/71 she stood off St Vincent when a local volcano threatened to erupt. She undertook Cod War patrols in 1972-3. In 1973 she became the original HMS HERO in the BBC TV series. She was fitted with Exocet at Devonport in 1975-7 and was fitted with a towed array sonar in 1982-4. In 7/88 she led the SAR operation when the Piper Alpha oil rig exploded in the North Sea. Paid off at Devonport 31/12/90, and was towed from Portsmouth 13/10/92 for breaking up in India.

HMS PORTISHAM

The Ham class inshore minesweeper PORTISHAM was one of the all wood construction vessels of the class - distinguished by the rubbing strake on their hulls. She was built by the Dorset Yacht Company in 1956, then placed in reserve until brought forward for the RN Auxiliary Service (in 1964) with her gun and minesweeping gear removed. She was sold to Suttons Boatyard in 11/69.

HMS PUNCHESTON

The PUNCHESTON was completed by Richards Ironworks at Lowestoft 20/9/57. She served in the Mediterranean and later in the Fast East, where she came under fire from an Indonesian shore battery in 1966. In 1967 she transferred to the Persian Gulf - note the pendant numbers on her stern in two languages. In 5/67 she formed part of a naval presence off Mukalla after an attack on the British residency. In 1971 she returned to the UK. She was sold to Pounds 5/72 and broken up at Dartford 1977.

HMS RECLAIM

The RECLAIM was a Diving and Submarine Rescue Vessel, built at Renfrew and completed in 10/48. Her design was based on the King Salvor Class of Ocean Salvage Vessels. She had reciprocating engines giving her a speed of 12 knots. She was based at HMS VERNON (Portsmouth) when first completed, but later operated from HMS LOCHINVAR at Port Edgar as a Minecountermeasures Support and Diving Trials ship. Later ABDIEL took over her minecountermeasures support duties and she concentrated on her diving role. She was replaced by the MV SEAFORTH CLANSMAN. Broken up at Bruges in 1982.

RFA REGENT

The Fleet Replenishment Ship REGENT was completed in 1967 by Scotts. She could carry a wide range of stores in her 18,029 ton (gross) hull, and could steam at 20 knots. In 1974 she helped evacuate British nationals from Cyprus; in 1982 took part in the Falklands War; and in 1991 was deployed to the Eastern Mediterranean in support of ARK ROYAL during Gulf War operations. She paid off 11/92 and sailed 25/1/93 from Devonport under her own power for breaking up in India.

HMS REPULSE

The nuclear powered, polaris armed submarine REPULSE was launched on 4/11/67 and completed on 28/09/68 by Vickers-Armstrongs at Barrow. The second of the four Polaris submarines to complete, she and her sisters maintained the deterrent patrol until the 90s, REPULSE returning from the 200th Polaris patrol on 23/07/90. She went on to complete the last Polaris patrol on 13/05/96, having conducted 69 patrols in her 28 years service, and covered 158,000 miles. She paid off at Faslane 28/8/96 and then sailed to be laid up in Rosyth.

HMS RESOLUTION

RESOLUTION was the first Polaris fitted submarine built for the Royal Navy, being launched by Vickers-Armstrongs on 15/09/66 and completed 02/10/67. Her 16 A3 missiles were upgraded with Chevaline warheads in 1984. She paid off on 22/10/94, having been run on an extra few months due to a delay in the Vanguard class programme. She completed 60 patrols, including the longest deterrent patrols of over 100 days. She was then laid up at Rosyth.

HMS REVENGE

REVENGE was the last of the Polaris nuclear submarines built, a fifth boat being cancelled. She was completed by Cammell Laird on 4/12/69. She had her missiles upgraded with Chevaline warheads in 1988. She paid off in 5/92, and was laid up at Rosyth, having covered over 400,000 nautical miles during 56 patrols. The Polaris submarines were able to sustain their heavy patrol cycle by the use of two crews, each of 141 officers and men to each operational vessel.

HMS RHYL

The RHYL, a Rothesay class frigate, was completed by Portsmouth Dockyard 31/10/60. She served in the Far East and Mediterranean and carried out Beira patrols, assisted during unrest in East Africa in 1968 and the West Indies in 1969. She was refitted with a flight deck 1970-72, but is photographed here at Malta in her original guise, with a single gun and twin mortars aft (contrast with photographs of ROTHESAY). She undertook Cod War patrols, and in 1974 assisted in the evacuation of British nationals from Cyprus. Paid off in 1982 and sunk in 8/85 when used as a target for guided missiles in the Atlantic.

HMS ROTHESAY

The ROTHESAY was built by Yarrow, completing 23/4/60. She was the first of her class to be modified - in 1966-68. In 1969 she landed troops in Anguilla. She undertook Cod War patrols 1973, and a Gulf Patrol 1981. In 1985 she was refitted for a new role in the Dartmouth Training Squadron. She paid off 31/3/88, by which time she was limited in her seagoing role. She had steamed 800,000 miles and served worldwide - winning the Colossus gun trophy 2 years running. She was towed to Spain for breaking up 1/11/88.

HMS SABRE

SABRE was a Fast Target Boat built by Vosper Thornycroft in 1970. Capable of 40 knots on her gas turbine engines, with Foden diesel engines for cruising. She was unarmed. She damaged her bow when hitting a breakwater in the Channel Islands in 1980, and was sold in 1983. Refitted and resold, she became the Greek EL CONDOR in 12/86.

HMS SALISBURY

The aircraft direction frigate SALISBURY was completed at Devonport Dockyard 27/2/57. In 1961-2 she was modernised with 965 radar fitted on a plated in "mack" aft. In 1967 she stood by during disturbances in the West Indies. In 1967-70 was refitted with Seacat missiles. In 1975 she completed the last Beira patrol. She undertook Cod War patrols in 1976, and was in five collisions with the gunboat TYR on 1/4/76 and two with the AEGIR 20/5/76. Later in 1976 she sailed for the Mediterranean during negotiations for her sale to Egypt, but eventually returned to UK the sale having fallen through. From 1980-5 she was a harbour training ship at Devonport. Was towed out and sunk as a target 30/9/85.

HMS SANDPIPER

The SANDPIPER was a Patrol Boat built on the lines of RAF rescue craft. Of 190 tons, she was driven by two Paxman diesels giving her a speed of 21 knots. She was completed in 1977 by Richard Dunstan, and was given an enclosed bridge whilst employed as a training tender to BRNC Dartmouth. She was sold to a Dutch company in 4/91 and was for resale at Rotterdam in 10/93.

HMS SCARBOROUGH

The Type 12 anti-submarine frigate SCARBOROUGH was completed 10/5/57 on the Tyne. In 1962-64 she was refitted for the Dartmouth Training Squadron with extra boats and a deckhouse aft. She retained her original small funnel throughout her service. Laid up in 1972, a proposed sale to Pakistan was not completed. She was broken up at Blyth 31/8/77.

HMS SCEPTRE

The SCEPTRE was commissioned on 14/02/78, having been launched by Vickers-Armstrongs at Barrow 20/11/76. She was the 4th of the S Class nuclear powered Fleet submarines, armed with five torpedo tubes and with good endurance and speed. The class proved very successful and were succeeded by a further development in the T class. They are, however, aging, but the first of their replacements, the A Class, were only ordered 03/97.

HMS SCIMITAR

The SCIMITAR was a Fast Training Boat of 102 tons, built by Vosper Thornycroft with a hull of glued laminated wood construction. Developed from the Brave Class, this class were unarmed. In 1979 she was taken to Hong Kong onboard MV HAPPY PIONEER to assist the local garrison during an influx of illegal immigration. Returned to the UK in 1981. She was sold to Greek interest in 1983 and renamed AQUILON.

HMS SEALION

The SEALION was the last of the Porpoise class diesel electric submarines built, completing on 25/7/61 at Cammell Laird's. A very successful design, and repeated in the Oberon Class, they had a dived speed of 17 knots and were armed with 8 torpedo tubes. She was at the Jubilee Review at Spithead in 1977. SEALION paid off 18/12/87 and was sold to the Charity "Inter Action" for display in London but was laid up at Chatham when the venture collapsed. She was towed to Blyth on 26/3/90 for breaking up.

SETTER

The SETTER was one of the many Dog class tugs used by the RMAS. Powerful and manoeuvrable, they were fitted with firefighting equipment but not with towing winches. Their masts could be lowered for working close under ships with overhanging sides and equipment, and they proved very useful in day to day dockyard work. SETTER was built in 1969 at Appledore and was based at Chatham and later Portsmouth, being operated by Serco-Denholm under contract after 1997.

RFA SIR BEDIVERE

The SIR BEDIVERE is a Landing Ship Logistic, originally of 6400 tons (gross) with the capacity to carry 340 troops, or 534 under austere conditions. Diesel driven and capable of 17 knots, she was built by Alexander Stephen in 1967. In 1970 the RFA took control of her from the BISN Co who were operating the LSLs for the Army until that time. She took part in the Falklands War. In 1990 she carried out a 12 tank lift to the Gulf, and served in the Gulf War 1991. She started a SLEP refit in 11/94 at Rosyth during which her hull was extended by 13m (39 ft) and she was given a new superstructure, new engines and power plant.

HMS SIRIUS

The SIRIUS was built in Portsmouth Dockyard, completing 15/6/66 - the last ship built there. She was a Leander Class frigate, fitted with Y136 machinery. In 1970 she won the Wilkinson Sword of Peace for her work in rescuing 100 survivors in the St Kitts ferry disaster. She was fitted with Exocet missiles in 1975-7, and refitted again with towed array sonar 1981-3. In 1988 she visited Australia during the Centennial celebrations there. She paid off 27/2/93 and was towed to Milford Haven 7/96 for use as a target.

RFA STROMNESS

The Stores Support Ship STROMNESS was launched 16/09/66 by Swan Hunter and displaced 12,381 tons (gross). Diesel driven and capable of 17 knots, she had a flight deck for vertrep work, but no hangar. She was at the Jubilee Review in 1977. She took part in the Falklands War. She was lent to the US Navy in 4/83, and sold to them 13/12/83, becoming USNS SATURN of the US Military Sealift Command.

HMS STUBBINGTON

The STUBBINGTON was built by Camper and Nicholson, completing in 7/57. She then served in the Mediterranean and at Aden. In 1967 she was deployed to Cyprus during a threatened Turkish invasion, and the next year assisted in earthquake relief in Sicily. In 1969 she became a navigational training ship at Portsmouth, and was the RNR MONTROSE 1972-76. After a refit in 1977 she joined the Fishery Protection Squadron. She paid off in 1986 and was placed in the Stand by Squadron before being broken up in Bilbao 9/89.

HMS TARTAR

The TARTAR was a Type 81 general purpose frigate built at Devonport Dockyard, completing 26/2/63. In 1975 she gave a demonstration of weapon firing to visitors in the Royal Yacht during a visit to Mexico. She undertook Cod War patrols in 1976, colliding with the gunboat TYR twice on 1/4/76 and the AEGIR on 22nd and 26th May. Her 4.5 inch guns were originally from old destroyers, and were sent to Aberporth in 1980 when she joined the Standby Squadron. She recommissioned to fill gaps in the Fleet after the Falklands War, and paid off 29/3/84. She was sold to the Indonesian Navy, refitted at Southampton 6/84 and was renamed HASANUDDIN 16/10/85.

HMS TENACITY

The TENACITY was a larger version of the Brave Class FPBs, being 165 tons to their 89. She was built as a private venture by Vosper Thornycroft in 1969, and purchased by the Royal Navy in 1972 after two periods of charter in 1971. She was fitted with three gas turbines giving her a speed of 40 knots, and diesel engines for cruising. She was used for exercises and for fishery protection duties, and also assisted with anti-terrorist operations in Northern Ireland. She was discarded in 1985, and sold. She was under conversion to a yacht at Portishead in 1996 when fumes from a chemical works stopped progress.

RFA TIDESPRING

The TIDESPRING was built by Hawthorn Leslie, being completed 18/1/63 as a later Tide class Fleet oiler, with flight deck and hangar. With a capacity to carry 17,400 tons of FFO and 700 tons of diesel, she was later adapted to carry 14,300 tons of diesel, 100 tons of lub oil, 2,100 tons of Avcat and 450 tons of water. In 1973 she aided the island of Rodriguez after a hurricane. She was at the Jubilee Review in 1977, and took part in the Falklands War in 1982, being part of the force that retook South Georgia. In 1991 she visited Murmansk and Archangel on the 50th anniversary of the Russian convoys celebrations. Paid off 31/12/91, she was sold for breaking up and left Portsmouth under tow for India 20/3/92.

HMS TIGER

The TIGER completed on Clydebank in 03/59 having been laid down 18 years earlier. She carried out several commissions as a gun cruiser, which included one in the Far East at the start of the Brunei/Borneo operations in 1962/63. She was also used as a conference centre for the Rhodesian (UDI) talks at Gibraltar in 12/66. She was converted to a Command Helicopter Cruiser at Devonport between 1968-72, as seen in this photograph. She was Flagship of the Second Flotilla for the Jubilee Review in1977, and paid off in 04/78 and laid up. She was broken up in Spain in 09/86.

HMS TORQUAY

The TORQUAY was a Type 12 anti-submarine frigate built by Harland and Wolff and completed 10/5/56 - the first of her class. She was refitted for the Dartmouth Training Squadron in 1962. In 1970-2 her after deckhouse was extended, she was given an enclosed foremast and taller funnel, and was used for navigational training and trials, and also for training Engineer Officers. She undertook Cod War patrols in 1976. She was paid off 31/3/85 and then sold being towed from Portsmouth 1/7/87 for breaking up in Barcelona.

HMS TRIUMPH

The TRIUMPH began her career as a light fleet carrier, launched by Hawthorn Leslie on the Tyne in 10/44 and completed in 04/46. After service as a trials and training carrier, she served in an operational role off Malaya and later during the Korean War. She carried out trials of the angled flight deck before being converted to a Cadets' Training Ship, relieving the cruiser DEVONSHIRE in 1953. She paid off in 12/55. and later started a £10 million conversion at Portsmouth for her 3rd role - as a Heavy Repair Ship. She commissioned in 1965, being based at Singapore until she returned to Chatham to pay off in 1972. She lay in reserve until 12/81, when she was towed to Spain to be broken up.

HMS UNDAUNTED

The UNDAUNTED was completed as a U class emergency war design destroyer in 03/44 by Cammell Laird. She served in operations off Norway and at Normandy in 1944 and then joined the British Pacific Fleet for operations against the Japanese. She underwent full conversion to a frigate in 1952/3. Here she is photographed as a frigate, with a helicopter deck aft, Limbo A/S weapons and a deckhouse in place of her twin 4 inch gun. She paid off as Leader of the 2nd Training Squadron in 1973, and was used for Exocet trials in 1974, later being sunk in 11/78 South West of Gibraltar by missiles fired by HMS NORFOLK and a torpedo from HMS SWIFTSURE.

HMS VALIANT

The VALIANT was launched on 3/12/63 at Barrow, and completed 18/7/66. She was the first all British designed nuclear submarine. She displaced 4,400 tons and was armed with 6 torpedo tubes. In 4/67 she completed a 12,000 mile, 28 day submerged voyage from Singapore to the UK, a record for a British submarine. She was at the Jubilee Review in 1977, and was one of the submarines that took part in the Falklands War in 1982. Whilst returning from the USA in 6/94 she developed engine problems and paid off 12/8/94 at Devonport.

HMS VENTURER

The VENTURER was built in 1972 as the stern trawler SUFFOLK HARVESTER and chartered 25/11/78 as an Extra Deep Armed Team Sweep Vessel, being converted at Lowestoft. She and a sister ship, the ST DAVIDS, were manned by the RNR, VENTURER being in the Severn Division. Of 392 tons, they had a speed of 14 knots, and worked as a pair. They were returned to their owners in 3/84 and converted to North Sea Standby Safety Vessels.

HMS WAKEFUL

The tug SWEDISH HERCULES (later DAN) was built in Selby in 1965, and purchased by the Royal Navy in 1974, for use in the Clyde as a submarine tender. She was also used on fishery protection duties, and on patrols to prevent the smuggling of arms or personnel into Northern Ireland. She paid off 30/10/87 after being relieved by the SENTINEL, and was sold to Hellenic Salvage Tugboats 06/88 and renamed AEGEAN PELAGO.

HMS WATERWITCH

The WATERWITCH had been built as the Inshore Minesweeper POWDERHAM by Samuel White at Cowes, completing in 1960. She was converted for survey duties in 1964 and was based at Portsmouth. She was used, as a Port Auxiliary Service vessel, 1968-82 - still surveying. Unlike her sister, WOODLARK, she retained her black hull. In 1982 she became a tender to the RN University Unit, Liverpool, paying off in 08/85. She was sold that year (later resold) and in 1997 was at the Royal Dock South Shields awaiting preservation.

HMS WHITBY

The WHITBY was completed by Cammell Laird 19/7/56. She had an earlier form of enclosed bridge which differed from her sisters, and never had the after structure extended. She undertook patrols in the Cod War 1973, being in collision with the gunboat THOR 27/9/73. She paid off in 1974, and was broken up at Queenborough, being towed there 16/1/79.

HMS WILTON

The WILTON was a repeat of the successful Ton class coastal minesweeper design, built for the minehunter role with a fibreglass hull - the first such warship so built - with the reconditioned engines from DERRITON. Completed by Thornycroft 14/7/73. In 1974 she was part of the force sent to clear the Suez Canal, which had been blocked for 7 years. In 1984 she was part of the standby force assembled for mine clearance operations in the Gulf of Oman/Strait of Hormuz, waiting in the Mediterranean, and took part in mine clearance operations in the Gulf of Suez at the request of the Egyptian Government. In 1991 she became a training tender to BRNC Dartmouth, paying off 27/7/94 and laid up.

HMS YARMOUTH

The YARMOUTH was built by John Brown, completing 26/3/60. She was modernised 1966-8 - her new gunnery director and foremast can be seen clearly in this photograph. She then deployed to the Far East, including Beira patrol duties. She undertook Cod War patrols in 1973 and 1976, being in collision with the gunboats THOR (twice) and BALDUR, receiving severe damage to her bow. In 1978 she assisted with oil pollution clean up operations when the AMOCO CADIZ ran aground off Ushant. She served in the Falklands War 1982, assisting in the rescue of survivors from the SHEFFIELD and providing gunfire support in the final assault on Port Stanley. She paid off 24/4/86, and was sunk as a target 21/6/87.

HMS YARNTON

The YARNTON was launched 26/3/56 by Pickersgill. In 1965 she joined the Persian Gulf Squadron, and in 1970 stood by during a dispute over oil off Abu Musa. She was one of five of the class converted to patrol vessels in 1971 to serve at Hong Kong. She was refitted at Hong Kong with two 40 mm guns and an enclosed bridge. In 1984 she was employed on patrols against mass illegal immigration. Replaced by the Peacock Class patrol vessels, she returned to UK and was sold to Pounds in 1986.

HMS ZULU

The Tribal class frigate ZULU was completed by Stephen 17/4/64. The class introduced improved accommodation standards, including dining halls and air conditioning, to frigate size vessels. She was fitted with Seacat missiles amidships which can be seen in this photograph. Paid off to the Standby Squadron in 1979, she was brought forward during the Falklands War, and commissioned after a short refit. She was the guardship at Gibraltar, and then paid off again 30/3/84. She was sold to Indonesia, being renamed MARTHA KHRYSTINA TIYAHADU, and being refitted at Southampton 6/84.

INDEX

Note: All photographs are Official Royal Naval Copyright except those on pages:

41, 55, 81, 85, 97, 115, 123, 139 and 154 which are the copyright of Deryck Swetnam of Portsmouth.

Rear Cover - HMS ROTHESAY - See page 131.